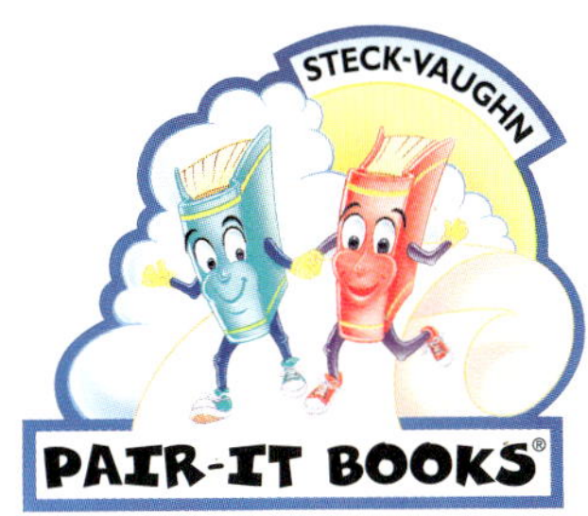

A Family Is Special

Written by Darwin Walton

www.steck-vaughn.com

A family has people special to you.

A family does many things together.
What does your family do together?

A family can cook a treat.

A family can sit together to eat.
Does your family do this?

A family can ride bikes.

A family can go for hikes.
Would your family like to do this?

A family can shop at a store.

A family can do many chores.
Does your family work together?

A family knows how to care.

A family knows how to share.
What does your family share?

A family can celebrate special days.

A family celebrates in many ways.
What does your family celebrate?

A family can have fun.

A family is special to everyone. Why is your family special?

A family has special people.